D0372080

Table of Contents

INTRODUCTION

The Sports Mindset Gameplan workbook is designed to provide you with the necessary tools to develop a positive mindset so you can perform in your sport with the highest level of confidence. The more you understand how you're uniquely motivated, the more you'll surround yourself with key components that will lead you to ultimate success in your sport and you'll enjoy your game as you never have before.

We created this workbook based on years of working with athletes to improve their mental game. You will learn how goal-setting, focus, and visualization, along with proper breathing and relaxation, can take your game to the next level and beyond. As you learn to develop a positive mindset and practice emotional control on a regular basis, you'll become a better player, with more confidence.

In a slump? Do you crumble under pressure? Do you have trouble bouncing back from setbacks quickly? Help has arrived! The Sports Mindset Gameplan will guide you through thought–provoking Focus Questions and Power Play Action Steps; both designed to give you crucial mental tools to get out of slumps and recover from setbacks quickly and efficiently. Most athletes enter competition with a physical and strategic gameplan. This workbook will provide you with a sports mindset game plan to go with it.

Or, are you a good player who is just looking for an edge in your sport? Putting extra effort and attention to the information in this workbook can not only give you extra tools to succeed, but inspire you as well.

We are committed to helping athletes gain mental strength, fitness, and toughness. You'll learn how to cultivate the same positive mindset as state champions, collegians, and professional athletes.

After completing the workbook, you'll have a strong gameplan for confidence on a more consistent basis.

For more information on what we have to offer, visit us at our website:www.spinw.com or give us a call at 866.300.1515.

Introducing the Sports Mindset Pyramid (SMP)

The sports mindset is positive. The sports mindset is relaxed. The sports mindset is focused. The sports mindset is confident. For athletes, mindset goes a long way. Athletes must be fully confident to perform at or even above their potential. This workbook will lead you up the Sports Mindset Pyramid: to learn the skills that build up to confidence. For now we'll briefly introduce the sport psychology techniques, and explain the steps necessary to make changes to cultivate and strengthen a positive, confident mindset.

"It's amazing how much of this is mental. Everybody's in good shape. Everybody knows how to ski. Everybody has good equipment. When it really boils down to it, it's who wants it the most and who's the most confident."
– Reggie Crist, professional skier

In sports, the older the athlete becomes, the higher level they achieve, the sports mindset becomes more and more important in distinguishing peak performance from average performance. In youth sports, the biggest, fastest kids are almost always "the best." But as players grow older and more experienced, the physical attributes start to balance the playing field, and the mental game often separates the good from the great.

The Sports Mindset Pyramid shows visually the components of the athlete's mindset. The tip of the pyramid is confidence. The building blocks that support it are the mental, emotional, and physical keys to achieving peak performance. As the blocks below it are strengthened, the more solid and predictable confidence becomes.

Recently, while working with an athlete whose goal was to earn a starting spot on his team, I asked, "What is the difference between a starter and a non-starter?" His answer was straightforward: "The starters are better players."

This illustrates the point that athletes know the best players in any sport are the most skillful, most athletic, and hardest working. But, what if you have two athletes who are equal in these three categories—who starts then? The answer may lie in the difference between the players' mindset.

In short, which one is more confident?

Confidence can be defined as:

"Having a strong belief in oneself and one's abilities."

Many people think of 'confidence' as being ready to play and compete at the highest level, but it is much more than that— confident athletes not only enter competition believing in their abilities, but also are confident they can break out of a slump or return to their highest level when things don't go so well.

The Sports Mindset Pyramid contains the mental skills athletes need to become and remain confident in their abilities. It is SPINw's belief that an athlete playing with confidence is more likely to enjoy the game and experience success.

The base of the sports mindset pyramid is skill, athletic ability, "sports IQ" and motivation to play, perform, and succeed. Through this workbook, we challenge you to use sport psychology skills to help improve not only your thought processes, emotional control, and mental toughness, but we also remind you to continually hone your talent and athleticism. Those talents can be enhanced and improved with a strong mental game. As you work your way up the pyramid, through the mental skills, keep this in mind.

Having a strong base to your Sports Mindset Pyramid is crucial. As the base skills separate good from great athletes, the sports mindset is what separates great athletes from the elite. In some cases, a strong mental game can propel a good athlete over a great athlete. Either way, the point is to allow you to perform up to your ability and beyond on a more consistent basis.

As we move up the pyramid, the mental skills are introduced. They are in an order designed to build on the last one. While the mental skills are all important, they build from most pertinent and general to more specific and advanced skills.

How to use this workbook

This workbook is broken up into levels to fit each individual athlete's needs. If something jumps out at you that you want to learn about and improve on right away, start there. Otherwise, this book is set in a logical progression, building from the base of skills to the tip of confidence. Go through the book chapter by chapter for a more holistic approach.

Focus Questions:

What do you hope to get out of this workbook?

How does your level of play change from practice to actual game time?

10

How quickly do you let go of mistakes?

Do you use your mistakes as learning opportunities, or do you beat yourself up?

Power Play Action Steps:

In the SMP below, on a scale of 1–10 (with 1 being very weak and 10 being very strong), rate yourself on each level at the current time.

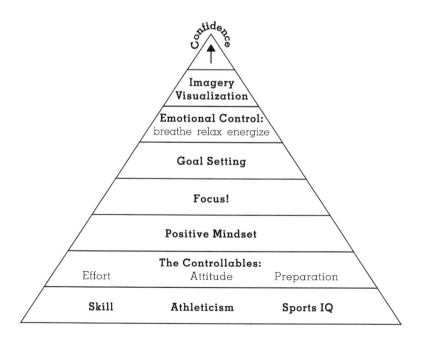

Level I – The Base: Skills, Athleticism, and Sports IQ

Utilizing sport psychology techniques and having a strong mental game are important, but they are no straight up substitute for what we will refer to as "the athletic base." No matter how confident, focused, and hard working you are, if you can't make a shot (skill), aren't quick (athleticism), or know the game (sports IQ), you are not going to be able to perform at a high level, no matter how mentally tough you are. As we mentioned in the intro, the difference between two players with the same skill level is the mental game, but let's make sure you have a good solid athletic base first and foremost.

The base blocks of the SMP are skill, athleticism, and sports IQ. As an athlete, you have a head coach, maybe some assistants or position coaches, strength and conditioning coach, and a sport psychologist (hopefully one from SPINw!) But you are also your own coach! You have a couple practices a week during the season but what about your days off? What about the off-season? What about when you are out with injury? You have to know what you need, how to do it, and when to do it.

So we'll now let you in on some coaching tips. In coaching team sports, the theory of "efficient training" means that coaches include these four components into training: technical, tactical, physical, and mental.

> **Technical** – Skills like: Ball control, puck control, swing, shooting, pitching
>
> **Tactical** – Strategies such as: Reading the play, help defense, when to make runs, game plan.
>
> **Physical** – Athletic traits like: Get faster, stronger, more agile, more flexible.
>
> **Mental** – Strategies to help: Focus, motivate, instill confidence.

As a mentally strong athlete who is now "self-coaching," these components are important for you:

> **Skill (technical)**
>
> **Athleticism (physical),**
>
> **Sports IQ (tactical), and the rest of the pyramid (mental).**

Focus questions:

What is your sport?

What position(s) do you play?

What are the technical skills required?

What physical skills are required to excel?

What tactical knowledge do you need to succeed?

Power Play Action Step: To help solidify the areas you need improvement on, ask your coach and at least one trusted teammate.

Let's look at each building block in the base separately. Many think that people are born with the base of the pyramid and don't stray too far from it. But those who have 'been there and done that' know that improvements can be made. For athletes with a good sports mindset, the first step is taking ownership of your skills, athletic ability, and sports IQ.

Block 1 – Skills

Elite athletes are highly skilled. In any sport, no matter if it's an individual sport like golf or swimming, or a team sport like football or basketball, having solid skills is crucial to performance and success.

Skills in sports can be broken down into specific physical techniques.

Here's an example:

Sport: Soccer   **Skill: Shooting**

Technique involved:

- **Plant foot: position and direction**

- **Kicking foot: Toe down, ankle locked, knee bent and over the ball**

- **Hips and shoulders: squared to target**

- **Body: leaning slightly forward**

- **Head: down**

- **Follow through toward target, land on the same foot you kicked with.**

If any of these technical pieces to the skill of shooting is off, that makes for an errant shot! To master the "Skill" of shooting takes hours and hours and hours of practice on the techniques until the body remembers the appropriate movements.

Practice makes proficient. Practice is more than just training. Working on your skills on your own is crucial for an athlete's confidence.

In his 2008 book, **Outliers: the Story of Success**, Malcolm Gladwell studied successful people in all fields and determined that "10,000 hours" of practice was the magic number for

> "The vision of a champion is someone who is bent over, drenched in sweat, at the point of exhaustion when nobody else is watching."
>
> – Anson Dorrance, head coach of 21 time national champion University of North Carolina women's soccer team

perfecting a skill. In one study of musicians, students were separated into 3 levels of potential as judged by their teachers:

Group 1– The most likely to be able to make a career in music

Group 2 – Somewhat likely to be able to make a career in music

Group 3 – Not likely to make a career in music

Of all the factors studied: talent, upbringing, socioeconomics, etc., none was more directly correlated to likelihood of making a career in music than practice time. Those who were "better" musicians had practiced more over the course of their lives than the others.

So with skill being one of the base blocks for confident performance, we say practice, practice, practice! Practice the seemingly insignificant techniques of the important skills. The more you practice, the more your confidence can grow.

What are 3 skills in your sport that you are proficient in?

Skill

Technique needed

Skill

Technique needed

Skill

Technique needed

18 *What are 3 skills in your sport that you need to work on?*

Skill

Technique needed

Skill

Technique needed

Skill

Technique needed

As you continue working your way up the pyramid, take special note of the following mental skills that can help with skill–building: Goal setting, visualization, and focus.

Block 2 – Athleticism

With this quote, do you see a similar theme with the skill segment? That's right – it's practice and hard work. There's really no secret to success! NFL Hall of Fame wide receiver Jerry Rice tops most all–time receiving statistics lists, but there are dozens with equal or better inborn athletic

ability. But practice and hard work helped to make him elite. Rice has a legendary work ethic – do you think there is any doubt that all the off–the–field work he did that no one saw helped shape his confidence on the field?

Here are some of the basic athletic skills required to perform at a high level of athletics.

Strength

Speed

Agility

Flexibility

Endurance

What are the 5 most important athletic skills required for your sport?

How do you rank yourself in each area on a scale of 1 – 10?

How can you improve in each area?

Block 3 – Sports IQ

Knowledge of your sport is another crucial element of performance. Being a "student of the game" can help push you to new heights. How do you "kill off a game" when leading in the final minute? How do you approach a certain opponent? These are the little details that can make the difference between a win and loss, or between giving yourself a chance to take the last shot or not.

Just after I graduated from college, I played in a local pickup soccer game with people from all walks of life: White, Black, Latino, European. Not only that, but there were people of all age ranges – from teenagers up to a few people in their 50s and 60s. Every now and then, we'd play the college/recently graduate players vs. the older guys.

One team of players who could run for days vs. a team with knee braces and grey beards. Who do you think won? If you said the college guys, have a seat. The old guys beat us every time! Why? We ran around like chickens with our heads cut off, thinking we were better than they were, trying to go it alone on the dribble and show off our skills, while the old guys calmly kept proper shape and positioning, controlled the ball, and picked the correct times to attack and score. In short, their collective "soccer IQ" was hundreds of points higher than ours. Here are a couple ways to improve your "sports IQ."

- **Know the history of your sport.**
- **Study players who have succeeded before you.**
- **Know the rules of your sport.**
- **Watch video and learn from it.**

Who is considered the best athlete in the history of your sport and why?

Which team is considered the best team ever in your sport? Why?

22

What are 3 things you know about your sport now that you didn't know 2 years ago?

Can you remember a situation in the past when "if you knew then what you know now", it would have made a difference in the performance or the outcome? Describe below.

What opportunities do you have to watch other athletes in your sport perform?

What opportunities do you have to watch yourself on video?

The Base is a Springboard to Confidence

The purpose of this workbook is to help you improve your confidence. If it's low, we'd like to get it up there. If it's high already, we'd like to keep it that way on a more consistent basis. Skills, athletic ability, and a high sports IQ form the base of the pyramid. The stronger you are at the bottom of the pyramid, the higher you and your confidence can go!

Faster than your opponent? More confident.

Stronger than your opponent? More confident.

Smarter than your opponent? More confident.

Better skilled than your opponent? More confident.

In better shape than your opponent? More confident.

This book was designed with individuals in mind. If you know the level you need the most work on, skip right to it and complete the rest of the book as you like. If you are not sure, just go straight through.

The Base Case Study

Lauren – high school lacrosse player

Lauren has been an athlete her whole life, but is new to lacrosse, having only started two years ago. She has made some high level teams, due largely in her opinion, to her athleticism, (she is bigger, faster, and stronger than her peers). She wanted to work with a sport psychology consultant because she was not playing well for her current select team. The reason being that she didn't feel like she was good enough.

As we examined the experience piece of it (she'd been playing a few years less than most players her age), we decided to look at the base. While her athleticism was her strength, we determined that to build her confidence, we needed to focus on:

technical skills (catching, cradling, and shooting), and sports IQ ("When people talk in lacrosse lingo, sometimes I don't know what they are talking about!")

Working on cradling would encourage her to hold the ball and make more runs. Working on becoming a better shooter would enable her to take more shots. Knowing the lingo would not make her feel quite as lost. As she set goals for the long, intermediate and short terms, these factors were worked in, and over time, she began to feel more confident in her abilities, increasing her playing time and enjoyment of lacrosse.

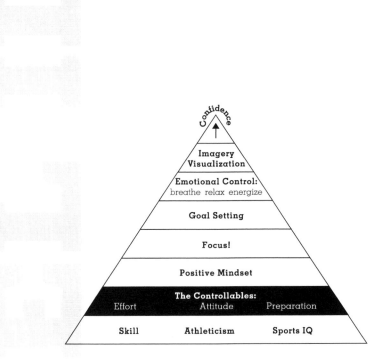

Level II – The Controllables:
Effort, Attitude, and Preparation

The athletic base can be looked at as the physical base.

Athletes need skill, athleticism, and sports IQ to be good

players. There may be certain limitations to them, but you can

push to maximize your potential and make the most of your

physical attributes. A good base of skill, athletic ability and

knowledge can be greatly enhanced by a strong mentality.

The second level of the Sports Mindset Pyramid is the basis

of all mentality for athletes – knowing and focusing on the

Controllables: Effort, Attitude and Preparation.

There are many factors in sports and life, and focus is a finite human quality. As you will learn more about in the Focus chapter, focusing on the things you have in your control is the most important key to the sports mindset, hence the Controllables being the first mental building block. So what are controllables? They are things that are 100% in your control. We will break these factors into 3 building blocks.

> "Because the talent level of most NFL players is so high, the question of greatness ultimately boils down to whether players "want to" do the things necessary to be great. Their work ethic and preparation are second to none."
> – Maurice Jones-Drew, NFL running back

Block 1 Effort:

In any situation in sports, effort level should be at the highest since you have control over that. If you are winning by 10, you can't control that, but you can control your effort. If you are losing by 10, you can't control that, but you can control your effort. If the referee has missed some calls, if you are not getting the playing time you think you deserve, or if it's raining, you can't control that, but you can control your effort level.

> "You can't just beat the person who never gives up."
> – Babe Ruth, major league baseball player

Effort in off–the–field daily life

Like with effort in training, effort in school, work, and everyday life is something that you can continually learn and improve on.

Part of building confidence is success, and this doesn't have to do only with your sport. Getting an A in a class that you've worked hard in gives you confidence. Earning a raise at a job you have worked hard at gives you confidence. Those types of successes are not held in a box but translate to your athletic situation as well. Make effort a habit.

What areas in your daily life require effort?

How would you describe your effort level for each?

How can you improve your effort level?

Effort in training

Coaches will often tell their athletes that 'you play like you practice.' You can't expect to put in half an effort in training and then automatically put in 100% effort in competition. Practice is not only for perfecting skills and getting in shape; it's engraining the way you want to play. A consistently high effort level is a big part of that.

Describe your general effort level in training:

How can you improve it?

Effort in competition

Effort in competition may seem like the easy part. And for the most part, it is. But what are the things that decrease effort in competition?

- Playing inferior competition (don't have to try as hard)

- Playing superior competition (see no reason to try)

- Losing and see no way of winning

- Bad calls by the ref

- Just not feeling confident

- Fear of failure

- No short term gratification

Describe your general effort level in competition:

What factors serve to decrease your effort?

How can you change your mindset about this?

Remember, how hard you work is 100% in your control. You have the ultimate decision whether or not to work hard in any given circumstance. Mentally strong athletes know what can potentially decrease their effort level, and take action to not let them.

Block 2– Attitude

Definition of attitude

"A mental position with regard to a situation."

What is your mental position or, 'mindset' most of the time? Is it different depending on the situation? Mentally tough athletes have the ability to stay positive and mentally tough no matter the situation. In other words, a good attitude at all times.

Things don't always go the way you planned. Most athletes are fine when things are going well, but what separates coming through in the clutch from choking is attitude. While it may not always seem like it, attitude is 100% in your control. No one person or situation has the power to change your attitude unless you let it. If your 'mental position with regard to a situation' is positive, you have a much better chance. While attitude is mostly an internal process (how you feel about a situation, and how you perceive that situation), it shows up externally two ways: body language and communication.

Body language

The way you hold yourself is the most efficient way to show your attitude. If you are playing well and winning, it's natural to walk a little taller, hold yourself upright, showing your pride, happiness, and all-around good feeling. If you make a few mistakes, it's easy to show a poor attitude by looking down, slumping your shoulders, and pouting. Which of these body postures communicates a mentally strong athlete?

Power Play Action Step:

Try this exercise right now. Stand up, and walk around the room like an athlete who has no confidence and a bad attitude. Describe the physical attributes you noticed:

Describe how it feels to hold yourself that way.

Now stand up and walk around like an athlete who is confident and has a good attitude. Describe the physical attributes you noticed:

Describe how it feels to hold yourself that way:

Okay, what was the difference? Did you feel differently about

yourself just by doing this little exercise? Most people are surprised when they do: attitude is supposed to affect body language, not the other way around, right? Remember this when in competition, training, and other areas of life. Holding yourself in a confident way can affect the way you feel! It can affect your confidence. No matter what the situation brings, you have 100% control over how you handle that situation. Learning to make positive body language a part of your character is a key to unlocking your confidence.

Communication: talking

The other way inner attitude is reflected to the outside world is how you communicate. When things are going well,

communication probably comes out with a positive bent: encouraging, informative, and directed. Example: "Good effort, but watch for the fake next time!" When things are not going well, communication can come out as negative, berating, or blaming. Example: "Why did you do that!? Don't fall for that!" Which instills more confidence in yourself and your teammates? The difference: a negative communicator points out the problem. A positive communicator offers a solution.

Name a time when your communication came from a negative attitude:

How would you have changed that if you'd had a positive attitude?

Communication: listening

Communication is half how you say things and half how you

hear them. Having a poor attitude can also influence how

you hear things. An athlete who is mentally weak and an

athlete who is mentally strong can hear the same exact set

of instructions from a coach in two different ways.

> **Example:**
>
> **Coach – "Hey! Find the pass quicker!"**
>
> **Athlete 1 (mentally strong, positive attitude): "Coach is right, he's trying to get the best out of me."**
>
> **Athlete 2 (mentally weak, poor attitude): "I was trying! Why is coach always getting on me? He hates me."**

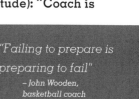

"Failing to prepare is preparing to fail"
– *John Wooden, basketball coach*

Name a time when you let someone's negative communication effect you.

Athletes need to have a deep belief that things will turn out well, no matter the situation. Maybe they will and maybe they won't, but having the right outlook or attitude, is the ONLY way to give it a chance to succeed.

Block 3 – Preparation

Preparation can be defined as "Doing all you can to be ready physically, mentally, and emotionally for training and competition." There is so much that athletes can do to prepare themselves for performing. Here is a comprehensive list – if you are not doing everything on it, make sure to add it to your routine.

Goals

We will go much more in-depth in the Goal Setting section of this workbook. But basically, athletes need to have clearly defined goals or objectives for the training or competition they are participating in. Knowing what you need to focus on before hand is key. Don't let situations dictate your focus.

Gear, weather and logistics

The little things are important. Where is practice and when? How are you getting there? What gear do you need? Is it washed? One of the surest ways to drive your coach crazy is to show up late, bring the wrong uniform, or forget a piece of equipment. If your focus is on finding someone to lend you an extra pair of shin guards or athletic tape, how much of your focus is now diverted from your upcoming competition?

In his book **They Call Me Coach**, John Wooden described how meticulously he showed his players how to correctly put on their socks, so that they would not be distracted by blisters later.

What about the weather? Will it be raining and will you need rain gear or different shoes? Will it be 20 degrees and you need extra layers or a heavy coat? Will it be 95 degrees with 90% humidity and you need extra water?

Having your plans and gear ready in advance ensures that you can put your energy and attention to your performance.

Rest and Nutrition

Picking up where we left off from the logistics and gear section, if it's going to be hot and humid, make sure you drink enough water the night before the game. Taking care of your body requires a little bit of attention. Why leave anything to chance?

Getting enough rest and proper nutrition are crucial to sport performance, and you have 100% control over them.

Training

Practice like you want to play. Also, see above: Effort in Training

Pre-training and Pre-game routines

All athletes know the importance of stretching and warming up before the game physically, but how many properly warm up mentally? There should be a mental component to your pre–game warm–up. When you warm up and stretch, you are transitioning your body from low energy to high energy, your muscles from tight to loose, your heart rate from low to high, and your lung capacity from normal to high.

What about your mentality? What about going from low intensity to high intensity? Going from no contact to high contact? What about the lowering of rationality and the raising of emotions? These are the things you need to "warm up" in your mind.

As you progress through the workbook, pay special attention to the mental building blocks: positive mindset, visualization, emotional control, and goal setting. A solid pre–performance routine adds these mental aspects to your physical warm up.

Can you name a time when your lack of proper preparation affected your performance?

How would you change that if you could go back?

Where are you already strong in your athletic preparation?

Which areas can you strengthen?

When you control the controllables, you leave only the game to think about, leaving you more able to handle the uncontrollable events that will undoubtedly arise in competition. Ensure you enter the game with confidence by controlling those factors that are 100% in your control.

Now you have a solid idea of your physical base, as well as the first rule of athletic mindset: Control the controllables. Read on to continue to strengthen and enhance your mental game.

Control the Controllables Case Study

Jennifer – high school track runner

Jennifer is a multi-sport athlete whose main sport is track. She has always been the fastest girl in her town. She wanted to work with a sport psychology consultant because she found herself in a "no-win" situation in her track career: everyone expected her to win, so if she won it was considered no big deal, but if she lost she was hounded by questions like "How did you lose?" "What happened?"

Her focus has recently started to drift towards other runners, fans and coaches, and failing to reach her time goals – in short, all things that are out of her control. We talked about how, by focusing on all those things that she can't control, Jennifer was stressing herself out! She got herself mentally worked up over all the things that might happen, and forgot about just performing at her best.

We worked together to shift her focus to those things in her control:

Attitude – Instead of getting down about what might happen, I challenged her to take on a more positive outlook, to stand tall and only talk about positives. Effort – Not that Jennifer's effort had been bad, it just wasn't 100% because of all the distractions. She improved tremendously on directing her focus away from questions and on to the effort necessary to obtain the high level of performance she wanted.

Preparation – Jennifer added a "mental warm up" to all her pre–practice and pre–race physical warm-ups that got her ready to compete to the best of her abilities. Through some hard work and dedication to changing her mindset, Jennifer started winning races again and renewed her passion for running track.

The Controllables:
Effort · Attitude · Preparation

Skill · Athleticism · Sports IQ

LEVEL III – Positive Mindset

Elite athletes are optimists. They believe that things will work out. They can see past adversity and stay focused on their goals. They focus on things they want to achieve, not the obstacles keeping them from succeeding. They think positive, speak positive, and act positive.

Positive does not necessarily mean the "Rah rah, you can do it," positive, although that is definitely part of it. Positive means confident, assured, definite, clear, and precise. Being positive is knowing what you want to happen, and not hoping that what you don't want to happen won't happen. To illustrate the point, take a moment to clear your mind, and then follow these directions: Ready? Okay, now whatever you do, do NOT think about a purple kangaroo. What's the first thing you thought about? If it was a purple kangaroo, why? I told you NOT to think about that! The reason

is that for the human brain to not think of something, it has to construct what that thing is, and then it can focus on something else. In sports, it's the same thing – when thinking thoughts like "I hope I don't miss," your brain hears "miss" first, thinks about what a miss looks and feels like, and then hears the "not." But by then it's too late! You need to think positively, such as "make it" or "follow through" – something that is positively-framed. If the base of your pyramid is solid and you've practiced a skill, trust that your body can carry out the technique necessary to complete the task at hand.

Peak performance starts with the first two building blocks: confidence in your abilities and controlling the controllables. If your skills are refined, you are in great shape, you've prepared for training, and your attitude and effort are good, confidence is bound to follow. But situations that are out of your control are bound to arise. On a rational level, most of us know what to do and the best way to react in any situation. But in the heat of battle, emotions run high and thoughts can turn panicked and negative.

So how do you cultivate and maintain a positive mindset?

The philosopher Aristotle said, *"You are what you continually do."* To cultivate a positive mindset, you must continually act in a positive way. Actions begin in the mind.

You may have seen this poster in school:

Watch your thoughts, for they become words.

Watch your words, for they become actions.

Watch your actions, for they become habits.

Watch your habits, for they become character.

Watch your character, for it becomes your destiny.

So the athlete you are destined to become is based on who you are (your character). Your character is based on those things you continually do (in other words, your habits). Habits come from actions, which come from words, which start as thoughts. Start with your destiny in mind and work backwards. Keep this in mind for goal setting (Chapter 5), but let's jot down a few ideas here first.

What do successful athletes in your sport continually do?

What negative habits do you have that you need to change?

What positive habits do you have that you should continue?

What factors make your thoughts or words negative?

To get you started building positive habits, complete the following 6 exercises to consistently live positive thoughts, words, and actions.

Positive Mindset Exercise 1:

The Positive Declaration

As the school poster says, everything starts with thoughts, so let's start by examining your thoughts about yourself in life and in sports. We will use the information below to come up with a Positive Declaration. A declaration is a positive, specific, and formal statement of fact. A good declaration starts with "I" and is followed by an active word like "will" or "can" or "compete".

Fill out the charts below, starting broad and simple and moving toward narrow and specific.

List 5 Positive Attributes you Possess

List 4 Successes You've had in Sports

List 3 Positive Statements about Yourself that You Know to be True

List 2 Positive Things you have Heard Someone say About You

47

Write a Positive Declaration, using the Qualities Above
(Remember to start with "I" and then a positive action word)

This positive declaration is like a personal motto. You are never

as bad as your worst mistake, although sometimes it may seem this way in the emotion of the moment. However, mentally strong and confident athletes know that one play does not define them. Your positive declaration is a statement that is generally true about you. Say it to yourself often to stay positive and confident during training and competition.

Positive Mindset Exercise 2:

Past Peak Performance

Now that we've brought your thoughts to the forefront, let's think about your positive actions. One of the greatest builders of confidence is past success. Let's take time to really dive in to your past success.

Do you remember your past peak performance? Not necessarily a win or a time when your team played well, but your best personal performance.

Power Play Action Step:

Take a minute or two away from the workbook. Close your eyes, take a couple deep breaths, and re-live that performance in your mind's eye as if it were a home movie. Pay close attention to the thoughts you were thinking, the emotions you were feeling, and any physiological sensations you experienced.

*Draw a picture of the event and describe the situation, including:
How did you feel?*

What thoughts were you thinking?

What did you learn from the experience?

When you were reliving that experience, did you feel like you

were there? Were you feeling good and even smiling? That's

what a positive mindset feels like. Remembering a past peak performance is about as positive as you can get. Also, know that if you are asked to do this exercise again in a year or two, let's expect the memory to be a different one – an even better performance!

Positive Mindset Exercise 3: Positive Self-Talk

In the first two exercises, we've analyzed thoughts and feelings about ourselves and positive success. Let's move on to our words. The way you think becomes what you say,

and we can look at your words in two ways; the things you say to others, the things you say to yourself. In the Attitude section of the Controllables level, remember that athletes with a weak or negative mindset point out problems, while those with strong or positive mindset communicate solutions. Positive communication is encouraging, and contains relevant information and direction.

Now let's shift focus to what you say to yourself - maybe not aloud, but the words you think – which we'll refer to as "self–talk."

Self–talk is the constant internal dialogue in the human brain. It can be positive (I am feeling great), negative (I am not looking forward to practice today), or neutral (I wonder what's for dinner tonight?).

"The Self-Talk Cycle"

In sports, self–talk can work in a cycle. That can be a good thing or a bad thing. In a good way, it keeps confidence high. In a bad way, it causes a slump. Having the mental strength to break out of a slump requires that you practice positive self–talk. Here are some examples. In the space below, write down how the self-talk cycle might influence the next similar action:

Action	Feeling	Thought Pattern	Self–Talk
Great shot	Great	Positive	"You're on fire! Keep it up!"
Missed shot badly	Negative	Negative	"That was awful, don't miss again!"
Air Ball	Negative	Positive	"More bend in the legs next time!"

For the second example, if we take it a bit further you can see a slump developing:

Action	Feeling	Thought Pattern	Self-Talk
Missed shot badly	Negative	Negative	"That was awful, don't miss again"
Air ball	Negative	Negative	"I missed again! What if we lose?"
Passes up open shot	Negative	Negative	"I can't shoot, I won't make it"
Taken out of game	Negative	Negative	"I will never play in college."

How would you expect this player to perform in the next game? We expect athletes to have a negative feeling when they miss a shot or double-fault on a serve. However, we also expect that their mentality is strong and positive enough to recover and not let the emotion take control. The thought patterns and subsequent self-talk need to be positive.

Here's another way to look at self-talk. It's a standard bit in cartoons: When the character is presented with a moral dilemma, there's a little angel version of that character on one shoulder and a little devil version on the other.

The devil says "Do it! You know you want to!" and the angel says "No, don't do that, it's not nice!" This is how it is for athletes – the devil tells you you're terrible and questions your abilities, while the angel builds your confidence and lets you know you can do it.

Who usually wins the battle? The one who talks the loudest, the one who talks more! So let's get the angel in shape by making him or her work on their stuff! The way to break a negative self–talk cycle or slump is to have the angel talk louder and more often.

When was the last time you remember negative self-talk (slump) affect your game?

How would you change that?

When was the last time you remember a positive self-talk cycle affecting your performance?

How can you ensure you do that on a more consistent basis?

Positive Self-Talk Strategies

Now you know the importance of self–talk being positively focused. Here are four strategies to use to help your angel win the self–talk battle:

> "Positive thinking is the key to success in business, education, pro–football, anything you can mention. I go out there thinking that I'm going to complete every pass."
> – Ron Jaworski, former NFL quarterback

Thought stoppage – Very simply, just stopping a negative thought. I've had athletes use a stop sign, the sound of a siren "the negative thought police" and the sound of their younger sibling yelling "Sttooppp!!"

Arguing – Rationally argue against the negative thought: When your little devil says "You stink!" your angel needs to step up the plate and argue your side "I am a good player, everyone makes mistakes. I will succeed next time."

Other side of the coin – Every event has two perspectives. Find the silver lining, see the glass as half full rather than half empty, or see the other side of the coin for that event. Instead of seeing how bad a situation is, see the good in it.

> **For example:**
>
> **Situation – Strike out**
>
> **Negative perspective – "A strikeout is the worst thing you can do!"**
>
> **Positive perspective – "Since I struck out, the pitcher and fielders might not be focused next time I'm up. I have the advantage next time up."**

Changing – For every negative thought, have a positive thought ready to change to. Use the strategies above to find the best way to change your negative thought to a positive as quickly as possible.

Now you try. Change the negative self talk below to positive self–talk using the strategies above.

Negative Self–Talk	"I stink!"	"Why did I do that?"
Thought Stoppage		
Arguing		
Other side of the Coin		
Changing		

Positive Mindset Exercise 4: My Thoughts

Write a list of your most common negative self–talk and then change the negative to positive.

Let's weed out all the negative thinking patterns that are ingrained in your head, and turn them around. In the chart below, start by becoming more aware of your self–talk tendencies.

Write in five negative thoughts that you have either said or heard. Then make those positive using one of the four skills we have learned.

For emphasis, negative thoughts are in lower case, but POSITIVE THOUGHTS ARE ALL CAPS!

negative thought	POSITIVE THOUGHT

Positive Mindset Exercise 5: Communication: Words

Yes, we covered this in the previous chapter, but it's so important, that we're going do it again using the positive mindset context. Remember that an athlete with a negative mindset is great at communicating problems. Those with a positive mindset find ways to communicate solutions.

Positive communication is: encouraging, informative, directive. Negative communication is: blaming, general, has the opposite effect of what was intended.

When was the last time you communicated negatively to a teammate?

When was the last time you communicated positively to a teammate?

Which of these was more effective?

When the word communication comes up, most people think of speaking – how you communicate verbally to others. That is half of it. The other half is how you listen and hear what others say to you. Remember that you cannot control others, so if a coach or a teammate is a negative communicator, there's nothing you can really do about it – you can't expect to change them (unless you buy them this book, which we highly

encourage!). But you can control your side of communication –
how you hear them.

To hear a poor communicator, you have to be mentally strong.
You can't take what they say or how they say it personally. A
positive communicator is like a miner panning for gold – you
have to sift through all the dirt to find the nugget of information.
If you can do that, you can then take the information and
choose to use it or not, but regardless, leave the emotion and
tone behind.

When was the last time you can remember someone communicating negatively to you that hurt your confidence?

What was the emotion that came through?

What was the information they were trying to communicate?

How could you have kept it from affecting your confidence?

Positive Mindset Exercise 6: Body Language: Actions

As your thoughts become words, become actions, become habits, your character will transform. Up to now, we have focused entirely on thoughts and words – which, with practice, will transform your habits and your actions will follow. But there is a way to have your actions positively affect your thoughts and feelings: Positive body language.

In the previous chapter you did an exercise where you walked around like a defeated athlete and remembered how it felt. For emphasis this time, draw a picture of that defeated athlete and describe each body part:

Head

Eyes

Shoulders

Arms

Feet

Does everything look 'down'? Does the body look 'slumped' over? Maybe this is where the term 'in a slump' came from...

Now draw a confident athlete. Describe.

Head

Eyes

Shoulders

Arms

Feet

For the confident athlete, everything is up. Being on a streak, a roll or 'on the rise' comes from this body posture.

Typically, low confidence means everything is down: Feet drag, shoulders slumped, eyes down ("don't look at me!"), while with high confidence everything comes up; bounce in your step, shoulders and head up, eyes straight ahead ("bring it on!"). While you were doing these exercises, did it make you feel and think differently? Usually we think of our body language as being a result of our mindset, and that is true. But not entirely true. You can change how you think and feel by how you carry yourself. Positive body language is a positive action. And making that positive action a habit changes your character. Positive character is a positive state of mind.

Create and Continue to Cultivate a Positive Mindset

As an athlete, you would probably describe your past peak performance as a positive experience in which your mindset was positive and you left the experience with a deeper sense of satisfaction. It is our hope that as you continue to grow in your sport, you hit those peak levels of performance more and more often.

You now have some skills to help you with positive thoughts, words, and actions, but these skills are nothing without practice and repetition. It's like shooting free throws: just knowing the techniques is not enough. It takes focused practice and repetition to make the skill second nature.

As you work your way up the Sports Mindset Pyramid to strengthen your confidence, make sure that being positive is a part of it. Here are the skills you have learned and will learn through a positive and negative lens.

Components of Sports Mindset	Positive	Negative
Confidence	Correct level of confidence	Unrealistically low (not confident) or high (cocky)
Visualization and Imagery	Positive images, seeing success	Negative images, fearful of outcome
Emotional Control	Use emotions to own benefit	Allow emotions to control and interfere with performance
Breathing	Deep controlled breathing	Shallow, not in control breathing
Focus	On factors that are in your control	On factors that are out of your control
Goals	SMART goals	Vague, unrealistic, and no time limit
Self Talk	"I can do this"	"We're going to lose"
Communication	Is helpful to teammates	Is not helpful to teammates

Which route will lead you to success?

Focus Questions:

1. On a scale of 1 – 10, rate your current positive mindset:

2. What is holding you back from fully having a positive mindset?

3. Which of the skills in this chapter will help you improve the most?

What is the most important thing you did today that proves you're working toward a positive mental mindset?

Melvin – high school basketball player

Melvin began working with a sport psychology consultant because he was experiencing some stress and loss of confidence moving into his junior year of high school. He wanted to make the varsity team, but wasn't performing well due to "psyching himself out."

After talking to him for an hour, I could tell that the lack of confidence was not limited to basketball, but his whole life! Although not in a bad way or on purpose, he was constantly portraying himself in a negative light: "I'm lazy." "Everyone at my school has something they do really well, but I don't." The first thing I challenged Melvin to do was to no longer allow himself to say these negative things about himself. It was such a habit and so unconscious at this point that I knew it would take a while, but that it could be done.

Together, we did all the exercises in this unit. He came up with a positive declaration: "When I focus and work hard, I am as good as anyone else." He determined the negative thoughts and self- talk that were not true and replaced them with positives, which I challenged him to use everyday.

65

With the positive thinking and self-talk, Melvin began to set higher goals for himself – not only for basketball, but for school and his social life as well. He ended up making the varsity team and enjoying playing basketball with less stress.

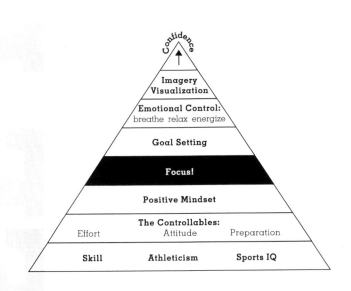

Confidence

Imagery
Visualization

Emotional Control:
breathe relax energize

Goal Setting

Focus!

Positive Mindset

The Controllables:
Effort   Attitude   Preparation

Skill   Athleticism   Sports IQ

LEVEL IV – Focus

"Focus!" "You're not focused!" "Stay focused!" "You've got to be focused!" If you're an athlete, you've undoubtedly heard some variation of these quotes many times. Sometimes it's not clear what that means, but the coach is probably trying to say, "Fully focus on cues relevant to successful performance!"

Let's start off with a sports definition of focus: "The ability to respond to relevant cues during training and competition."

> *"I think I've had somewhat pressure on me the last few years and I don't really ever think about it, because all I worry about is what I can control and that's my attitude, my effort and my focus. Those are all things that I can control – I can't control anything else, so I'm really not going to spend much time worrying about it."*
> – Tim Tebow,
> 2 x NCAA National Champion
> Heisman trophy winner,
> NFL Quarterback

The important word here is relevant. During training and competition, the athlete (and coach, and team as a whole) must know what the relevant cues are during that particular time. This unit is designed to help you focus on relevant cues as much as possible. Equally important to "focusing" is "re–focusing" which we will define as:

"The ability to return to relevant cues quickly when irrelevant cues are introduced during training or competition."

How do you do that though? Being able to focus, re–focus, and remain focused is not something that just happens; it is a process. The information and exercises in this chapter will give you some insight into the mind, and how to take control of your focus during training and competition.

Focus exercise 1: Focus on one thing

Get a stopwatch and set it for one minute. Close your eyes, hit start, and focus on your breathing until the watch beeps. Were you able to stay focused on your breathing for an entire minute?

What other things did you think about?

It's funny – everyone thinks they can focus on one thing for one minute, but this exercise illustrates how hard it actually is. Here's the trick: thoughts will pop into your head, and you will lose focus. The important thing is to be aware of this and be able to re–focus your attention to one thing, in this case breathing. So if another thought pops into your head, take notice, accept it, and remind yourself to re–focus on your breathing. Don't get mad at yourself or trip out on it, just take notice.

Now, set your watch for 2 minutes. Focus on your breathing for two minutes. Use the strategy above to re–direct your focus to your breathing.

Were you able to re-direct your focus?

Was it easier to focus than it was the first time?

Did your knowledge or awareness help you the second time?

The concept of focus seems like the simplest thing in the world. Just do it, right? But again, this exercise illustrates the power of the human brain and how difficult focus really is. Did one minute seem like an eternity? Now think about a 90–minute soccer game, a two hour tennis match, or a weekend–long tournament. Focus is hard. But then again, so is physical strength and fitness. Being physically fit takes energy, effort, and continual work. So does being in mental shape. Those who are mentally fit can stay focused for longer and regain lost focus quicker. The result is increased confidence and better performance.

Focus questions:

Can you remember the last time a "lack of focus" affected your performance in a negative way?

If you were able to go back and – do it again, – what would you do differently and how?

Breaking it down: Focus in four basic areas

Focus is such an abstract concept. It is hard to describe, but you know it when focus is correctly directed and when it's not. Let's take the time to break focus down into manageable chunks. Sport psychologist Robert Nideffer dissected focus across two axis into 4 areas:

> "When it comes to the football field, mind will always win over muscle and brute force."
> – Walter Camp,
> football coach, Yale

Internal

Narrow ──────────┼────────── Broad

External

Broad – Things at distance, everything taken into context, "the big picture"

Narrow – One specific element or aspect

Internal – Factors within yourself (confidence, breathing, positioning, etc)

External – Factors outside of yourself (the ball, teammates, opponents, the field, etc)

	Internal	External
Broad	Analysis of inside factors: Past experience, skill level, readiness	Assessment of outside factors: Field conditions, weather, opponents, obstacles
Narrow	Performance: Instinct, executing the task at hand	Finding the relevant cue: Ball, teammate, space in field or court

It is important to know each of the four factors. Different situations call for a different type of focus. Here is an example of shifting between all four categories of focus at the appropriate times:

Let's use a soccer goalkeeper for example:

She must have a broad/external focus when the ball is on the other side of the field (Where is the ball? Where are my defenders? Where is the next attack likely to come from? Where is the open space on the field? Where is the sun?)

She may shift to a broad/internal focus during this time ("If this situation arises, this is how I'll handle it." "I have been solid coming off my line lately and I am ready for it") as there is no direct action she must take, and she now has time to circle breathe, decompress, and mentally prepare for a shift towards her end.

As the ball gets closer to her, the focus must shift to a narrow/external focus (the ball is close to the box, keep my eye on it, ready for the shot).

As the shot is on its way, the focus becomes narrow/internal (techniques: moving her feet, hand position, body position).

Focus Questions:

1. Which of these four basic areas do you feel is the most important in your sport?

2. What are some factors in your sport that you must focus on in each quadrant?

	Internal	External
Broad		
Narrow		

What is the easiest for you to focus on?

What is the hardest?

Focus exercise 2: In vs. Out of Control

In the Controllables chapter, you learned that the controllables are Attitude, Effort and Preparation. We will take that idea a step further now and ask you to think about your sport and the factors involved: specifically what factors are important or relevant, and

"I'm trying to do the best I can. I'm not concerned about tomorrow, but with what goes on today."
    – Mark Spitz,
    Swimmer,
    Olympic gold medalist

which are not; which factors completely take your focus away,

and which ones keep you motivated and confident.

Power Play Action Step:

1. In the table below, write down which factors are in your control and which are not. For the In your control column, only write down things that are 100% in your control.

In Your Control	Out of Your Control

When your focus goes to things you cannot control, you are

wasting your energy! There is only so much energy to go

around, and thinking about, talking about, or being upset about

things that you cannot change is wasted energy. The faster

you can decide which in-your–control factor will help you, the

better. Control the controllables.

Focus exercise 3: *Internal and External Distractions*

The controllables are factors that are relevant to how you perform. They are the factors that you should take action on. Everything else is just a distraction. If we break up the word distraction, we get:

The prefix "Dis" which basically means "to pull apart"

And – "Action" – getting something done

Sports is all about action. Anything that pulls that action apart weakens it. So assuming you are participating in sports to get something done, let's drop the "dis!"

Athletes, like all people, are unique. A distraction for one athlete might not effect another athlete at all. So, it's very important to know what factors distract you personally.

Now, let's drill it down a little further to find the things that steal your focus: internal distractions and external distractions. Internal distractions are things within yourself (self–talk, injuries, attitude, etc.), while external distractions are things outside of yourself (crowd noise, weather, etc.)

Power Play Action Steps:

Think about the distractions you face in your sport, and fill out the table below:

Internal Distractions	External Distractions

Focus Questions:

Which of these distractions is the most common for you? Internal or external?

How can proper preparation help you better handle distractions?

How does having your attention scattered toward several activities at once contribute to your distraction level?

Focus exercise 4: Focusing cues

Now that you are aware of the factors that distract you and take you out of your game, let's combat that. In the Positive Self–Talk

section, you learned about "changing" or having a positive thought in your head ready to replace a negative thought that may come up. The same is true for focus – have an "in–your–control" thought ready to replace what's out of your control. You have your list of what's in your control and what's not, and you have thought of the main factors that distract you from your performance. Now, come up with focusing/re–focusing cues that can quickly replace them, and get you back on track.

A focusing cue can be a word, phrase, image, or action. Here are some examples:

Word: "Focus!" "Control"

Coach yourself – remind yourself that you are in control.

Phrase: "My goal is to…" "I am in control."

Positive Declarations and goals are a great way to re–focus.

Image: Making a shot, the ball

Positive imagery produces positive feelings and thoughts.

Action: snap, readjusting cap or socks, circle breathing

If a picture is worth a thousand words, an action is worth a thousand more. Adjusting your socks becomes more about function than fashion; it is a reminder that you are in control of your focus.

Brainstorm some ideas:

Word

Phrase

Image

Action

Come up with a focusing cue for each of your top three distractions:

Distraction	Focusing Cue
1)	
2)	
3)	

To focus, to re–focus, and to sustain focus, it is helpful to have strategies established and to practice them. To get in better shape you run sprints and do sit ups. To keep mentally fit, make re–focusing a priority. Do it in practice and training. Do it in school. Do it at work. Make it a goal.

Focus Case Study

Anthony – high school basketball player

I worked with a high school basketball team several years back and one of my athletes used this technique to perfection. The team was scattered overall (several transfers, no real natural leaders) and this athlete was the only sophomore on the team. Obviously a good player having made varsity at such a young age, he struggled to perform well, averaging about 4 points a game during the first part of the season.

As we talked, it came up that he was trying to fit in and was following the older players, checking out girls in the stands, trying to look cool, and other factors out of his control - distractions. We talked about focusing on the game and just doing the things he did to the best of his abilities. We talked about all the distractions he faced, and we came up with a focusing cue together: Before walking into the gym, he wiped his feet on the carpet on the way in the door to remove the distractions. With each swipe of his foot, he said "School", "girls", and whatever else was on his mind. He did not enter the gym until leaving those distractions behind.

Confident and focused, he walked into the gym and for a weekend tournament of 3 games, he scored 21 points a game and won the tournament MVP. He continued to use this and other strategies to stay focused, and entrenched himself as a starter and team leader as a sophomore. Anthony went on to earn a college scholarship.

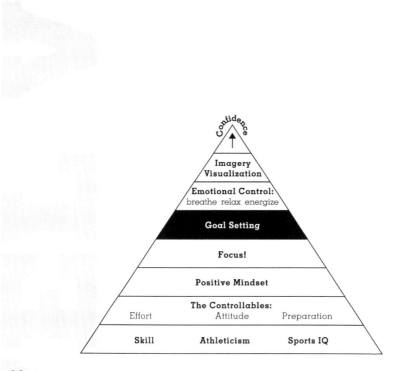

Level V – Goal Setting

We are now at Level 5, the Goal Setting step of the Sports Mindset Pyramid. If you look back at levels 1 through 4, you may understand the concepts, and see the destination you want to reach. But now you need a practical way to go about reaching that destination. Goal setting is the way. It's more than just a map – it's an itinerary, a back pack, and an encyclopedia. You may have heard the saying, "The journey of a thousand miles begins with a single step." I would contend that the journey starts even before that—with the idea that one wants to make that journey. Keep this in mind as you learn about setting goals for your sport.

One of the things that defines SPINw's hometown of Portland, OR, is Mt. Hood. About 60 miles from downtown, Mt. Hood is visible from many places in town. On a clear day, it is a pointy, snow-covered peak that seems to float above the ground. It is an oasis of calm outside of the bustling busy city, and many Portlanders—hikers, skiers and snow boarders, photographers, campers, and climbers among others—take weekend trips to get away from it all for a while.

As peaceful as it looks from a distance, its high elevations and unpredictable weather conditions make it treacherous and even dangerous. Every year it seems, some hikers or mountain climbers get lost and rescue teams are sent in to find them. Many more are able to reach the summit, or spend an incredible amount of time enjoying all that it has to offer.

As we start to think about goal–setting, we'll use Mt. Hood as our example. You see the top of this stunning mountain. You imagine to get there would be difficult and would take time but the feeling of accomplishment and the view from up there would make it all worthwhile. In sports, that is the essence of what you do: set your sights where you want to go and imagine what it would be like to get there.

If you were to ask 500,000 people in Portland if they'd like to get to the top of Mt. Hood, let's say 400,000 say, "yes." And then let's say that 10,000 attempt the climb, and even fewer make it. Why do only 500 (a fraction of 1%) of those who said, "yes", actually make it to the top? We could probably find similar numbers asking young athletes if they'd like to get to the Major Leagues. Many would say, "Of course!" But only a small percentage of those will actually put forth the focus and effort it takes, and an even smaller percentage will actually make it. This example of recreational climbing can be applied to sports. The journey (whether it's climbing Mt. Hood or setting a personal best in your event), might physically start with a single step, but mentally, it starts with the idea, and is set in motion by taking the action to set the goal, writing it down, and declaring a promise to yourself. It starts with having the idea, setting the goal, and carrying that goal to fruition.

Our definition of goal setting:

"Defining success, and taking the appropriate steps to achieve that success."

In the end, those with effective goal–setting plans give themselves the best chance to succeed at what they are doing. In this level, you will learn the ins and outs and finer points of goal–setting. At the end of this unit, you will have a blueprint for setting personal goals in your sport.

"Ready, Fire, Aim!"

Wait a second, that's not right! But athletes do it all the time, by stepping on the field not fully focused — without set goals—and then scratching their head at how it did not go the right way. To climb to the top of Mt. Hood, you don't just "fire" by walking toward it; you "aim" first, figuring out the right course. With the proper focus, and goals in mind, we all know the right way:

> **Ready (prepare, relax, and focus)**
>
> **Aim (narrow focus to what you want to accomplish, and nothing else)**
>
> **Fire! (Do it!)**

In the world of sport psychology, goal–setting has proven through research and practice to be an effective mental skill if done correctly. Anyone can set goals, but there are specific steps to setting them properly and effectively so that they can work for the setter, and not just hang in the air, unutilized.

Focus Questions:

So, what is your mountain or summit?

Define your success here:

Before we begin setting goals, let's explore the basics of what goal setting is, to erase any misconceptions and make your goals as effective as possible.

Goal Setting Basics: Who, What, When, Where, Why

Who should set goals? Anyone who wants to achieve something; anyone who wants to reach a destination.

What are goals? There are many ways to define goal setting, but for our purposes, it is: Defining success, and taking the appropriate steps to achieve that success.

When should you set goals? Goals can be set pre–season, before training and competition. Most importantly in the "when" category is that goals should be set continually. Set goals, reach destinations, and re-set your goals.

Where should you set goals? Do you make good decisions when you are relaxed or tense? Calm or excited? When you set goals, you are deciding how you are going to achieve success. That decision is best made in a calm environment when you can fully focus on it. Avoid setting goals directly after a tryout or a big win or loss when you are overly emotional.

Why should you set goals? Improve confidence, focus, and motivation. Decrease stress, de–motivation, and burnout.

Goal–Setting Basics Ready?

To begin to define what success is, you have to know where you are starting from. You need to know:

Where you've been

Where you are now

How you got where you are now

Where you want to go

Power Play Action Steps:

Write down a brief history of your participation in sports.

What type of player are you currently?

What are your strengths in your sport?
Skill I Athletic I Sports IQ I Focus I Positive Mindset

What areas do you need the most improvement in?
Skill I Athletic I Sports IQ I Focus I Positive Mindset

86

My Goals, 1st draft

Write down 5 things you'd like to accomplish in your sport:

Keep these in mind because we're coming back to them later.

Goal-Setting Basics: Aim

Now you are Ready (who, what, when, where, why), it's time to Aim. This is the 'how' of goal–setting. To aim, or actually set your goals, you must consider these 3 factors:

1) Goal Type

Outcome – Statistics goals. Winning, scoring, and anything with a number attached. Let's face it, at the end of the game there is a winner and a loser. Everyone wants to win, but not everyone can.

Performance – "How you perform" goals. Remember the second level in the Sports Mindset Pyramid – Attitude, effort and preparation? Performance goals are important because they shift your focus to the everyday effort and improvement of your performance; away from results and onto the things that make the results more likely.

Process – Skill–based goals. Remember the base of the Pyramid? Each skill is broken down into techniques. This is the most specific type of goal: how to improve on a skill by focusing on one technique at a time.

The most effective goal–setting plans are balanced between the three above. Outcome goals are great, but since they are not 100% in your control, they can often backfire; de–motivating, and in some cases can lead to burnout. However, outcome

goals are good to give you a reason to perform at your best.

Each individual athlete is different. Athletes tend to fall

somewhere on the spectrum below. Outcome oriented

athletes are driven to win and score and beat the opponent.

Performance oriented athletes are driven to improve and play

at their potential. Most athletes are driven by some combination

of both.

On the line below, put at X where you are.

| **Outcome** | _____ | **Performance** |
| **oriented** | | **oriented** |

A good goal–setting plan takes this into account and goals are

set accordingly. If you are driven more to perform, set more

performance goals. If you are driven to score and win, set

outcome goals. Everyone should set process goals! The best

goal setting plans include all three.

My Goals, 2nd Draft
Rewrite your 5 goals from the previous section and indicate whether they are outcome, performance, or process goals. Add a new goal or replace an original one if necessary.

2) SMART Goals

Goals are the most effective when they are set "SMART." Make

sure that your goals are:

Example	Good Goal	Not that Good
Specific	Specific objectives	"I want to get better and do my best"
Measurable	Athlete can definitely say yes or no	Achievement up to interpretation
Adjustable	Accounts for factors out of control	Does not account for out of control factors
Realistic	Challenging but within reach	Too hard, or too easy
Time-based	Time, day, week, date, etc. –specific	Open–ended

It's okay for goals to start out generally, but using the SMART theory, keep asking the question "How?" after you set your goal. If you can break it down further, keep going! Once you cant answer any further, that's a SMART goal.

> **Example:**
>
> **SPINw: What is your goal?**
>
> **Athlete: To get better at free throw shooting.**
>
> **SPINw: How?**
>
> **Athlete: By working on my technique?**
>
> **SPINw: How?**
>
> **Athlete: I need to keep my elbow in.**
>
> **SPINw: How?**
>
> **Athlete: By focusing on keeping my elbow in.**
>
> **SPINw: How?**
>
> **Athlete: By practicing more.**
>
> **SPINw: How?**
>
> **Athlete: I will take 100 free throws 3 times a week, focusing solely on keeping my elbow in for every shot.**
>
> **SPINw: Sounds like a really SMART goal.**

Now, let's see if this goal is SMART. Is it Specific? Yes. Measurable? Yes. Adjustable?

"As long as I am improving, I will go on."
– Mildred "Babe" Didrickson Zaharias, LPGA

Yes. Realistic? Yes. Time–

based? Yes.

By accomplishing this goal, will this player become a better free throw shooter?

My Goals, 3rd draft
Now you try! Rewrite your goals using "SMART" language.

3) *Time Period*

Goals will change over time. Let's take the hiking Mt. Hood

example. If your goal is to climb to the top, and you keep

looking up at the top, you may trip on a rock or a root right

below your feet. But if you are just looking down at the roots

and rocks on the trail, you may lose site of your motivation –

getting to the top of the mountain.

As with other areas of life, in sports it is crucial to start with the end in mind. First, figure out what is the ultimate goal, and then work your way backwards.

Making your goals SMART (still aiming!)

My Goals, Final Draft
Now write your SMART goals in a time–based order, from long term to short term.
Long Term –

Monthly – My goals for this month are...

Weekly – My goals for this week are...

Daily – My daily goals are...

Goal setting exercise 3: FIRE!

Congrats, you have your first goal–setting plan. Now it's time to fire – go out and execute! Now it is important to keep up with these goals. It's one thing to write them down one time and never look at them again. It's yet another to follow them, succeed in them, and then set new goals for the next week. Continue to set goals through out the season.

Remember the 'when' of goal setting is 'continuously'. Athletes should set goals each week. At the end of the week, check off the goals you've accomplished and set new ones. For each goal you were able to accomplish, figure out why you weren't able to accomplish, and use the SMART principle to adjust your goal to be able to achieve it next week.

Building and maintaining confidence is a continual process.
The best way to build confidence is through success.
Remember the definition of goal setting:
"Defining success, and taking the appropriate steps to achieve that success."
If you define success, and achieve that success on a daily, weekly, and monthly basis, that's a recipe for confidence!

Focus Questions:

1. What is your 'journey'?

2. What is your first step?

3. What is a good, consistent time to dedicate to goal setting?

Goal setting case study

Norman – Select Hockey player

Norman was a high school aged hockey player who had NHL ambitions. He was a high level player but a series of out-of-his-control situations in his life made it nearly impossible to perform up to the standards he was used to. To make things worse, since it was mainly a family matter, those things in his control - his effort, attitude and preparation – were not fully in his control for the first time in his life. He began working with me to try to figure out what to do.

The first thing we had to do was work really hard on setting his goals correctly – especially to factor in the A in SMART, the Adjustable part. On a side note, this is key with most high level athletes who deal with some type of setback – injury, politics, family situation, etc. – anything that's not in their control. They are so used to playing at a high level, that when they don't meet that level, they start to lose confidence. It was important for Norman to set SMART goals, keeping the end goal in mind. He just had to take a different path than he'd planned on for so long.

His long-term goal of making the NHL still stayed intact. But each week we had to adjust the monthly, weekly and daily goals. In the beginning, the daily goals were just to take control of his life off the ice. Breathing, relaxation, and positive self-talk techniques were crucial to his well-being. The weekly goals included being focused on only one or two things at practice or workouts.

As he started to re-gain control in his off-the-ice life, we began to focus on his base (skill, athletic, hockey IQ) goals, his on-ice mentality, and charting his path toward the NHL. Currently, Norman is still working on his long–term goal. He learned new skills off the ice that translated into his game. He has a new perspective on life and hockey that has improved his enjoyment of the game immensely.

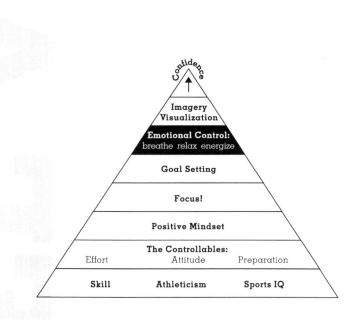

Level VI – Emotional Control

When thinking about sport psychology, most people think of, well, thinking! Mental toughness is more than having strong thoughts and being able to control how you think. It's equally or maybe more importantly about emotions. Think about it. Do you think confident? Or do you feel confident? So if the goal is full confidence, you have to be in full control of your thoughts and your emotions.

In the preceding levels, you have learned about your thought processes and now have some skills to control and focus your thoughts positively. But as in other areas of life, in sports, emotions are often more powerful than thoughts. The desire, the effort, and the competition of sport lends itself to a high level of emotion. Sometimes you need to raise your emotional level, and sometimes you need to lower it to compete at your peak level.

In this chapter, you will learn to become aware of emotions and how they affect your performance. Then you will learn the skills to help you control them.

Re–learning Anxiety

Athletes understand that, in addition to the skills and athleticism, there is a mind–body connection that goes beyond what the eye can see (otherwise, you would not have this workbook!)

Let's start by reviewing what you know (or think you know) about anxiety.

Briefly describe anxiety: what it is, what it feels like, etc:

Is anxiety a positive or a negative for athletes?

Anxiety is typically thought of as a negative – a situation that is stressful and unwanted. However, as a high–level athlete, it's time to un–learn that. Let's define anxiety as a higher vibration in the body and mind. From now on, look at anxiety not as a negative or a positive necessarily, but as neutral. It's just there. Your mindset and what you do with that anxiety is what makes it positive or negative.

We will call negative anxiety stress, and positive anxiety energy

Where does anxiety show up for you physically?

How does anxiety affect you mentally?

As an athlete, you know that a certain amount of anxiety is needed to perform at a high level. The trick is that you don't want to have too low of energy or too high of stress. So how to find the balance can be examined using the "Inverted U" theory. This is an old sport psychology theory that shows you graphically your "optimal anxiety level."

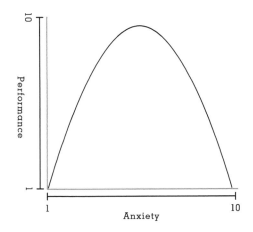

Before a big game, you might be anxious in a good way – excited for the game to start, or in a bad way – nervous that things might not go well. The Inverted U Theory says that, as your anxiety level rises, your performance rises also, up to a certain point, your optimal performance level. Once anxiety goes higher than that optimal level, your performance will begin to drop. Every athlete is different and the key is knowing yourself and what energy level you need to be at to perform at your best. Then come up with the skills that allow you to adjust your energy level during competition if necessary.

Name a player in your sport who performs at his or her top level when anxiety level is high?

Name a player in your sport who performs at his or her top level when anxiety is low?

What is your Optimal Anxiety number?

What factors can cause you to be at a lower level?

What factors can cause you to be at a higher level?

It is important to know what things tend to get you too high or too low. Being aware of these factors is key to finding the right skills to increase or decrease as need be.

The Controllables (again!)

Here's another reminder to focus on the controllables. The things that most often get us stressed are those things that are not in our control. Past mistakes, looking in the future (what if we lose?), and a referee's bad call – these are the kinds of things that raise anxiety, and are usually looked at as negative, thus producing stress. So here's another call to focus on the controllables.

But again, this is a rational solution. How do you go from an emotional reaction to logical thinking so that you can control your mentality? The answer starts with a simple process: breathing.

Breathing – a skill to live by

Breathing is the link between your conscious and unconscious mind. If you are not consciously thinking about your breathing, you breathe. However, if you think about it you can hold your breath, slow down your breathing, or speed up your breathing. A person can generally tell their emotional state by their breathing. If you are excited or scared (have a high level of anxiety), your breathing will be shallow and short. If you are asleep or meditating (low level of anxiety), your breathing will be deep and slow.

Before we go further into the importance of breathing for athletes, let's take a remedial science lesson and study the basics of breathing.

Scientific fact 1: Humans can live for about three weeks without food, three days without water, but only three minutes without oxygen.

Scientific fact 2: "Breathing is the process that takes oxygen in and carbon dioxide in and then out of the body."

Scientific fact 3: Oxygen is what your body needs on a cellular level.

Basically, the body takes air in through the mouth and nose into the lungs. From there, the lungs filter in oxygen, which is carried through the blood to your muscles and your brain, and filters out carbon dioxide, which leaves the body when you exhale.

Here are some forms of unconscious breathing:

Sigh – a deep breath to relieve frustration

Yawn – a deep breath when you are tired – triggered by lack of oxygen in the brain

Gasp – quick stoppage of breath due to fright

Pant – quick, shallow breathing for when you're tired

A good athlete can control their breathing. The most basic type of controlled breathing is circle breathing.

Circle Breathing

Circle breathing is a deep, even, slow, controlled breath meant to be efficient, while having a calming effect on both body and mind.

When athletes get tired, breathing can naturally become shallow and quick. This is your body's natural reaction of trying to "catch your breath." But remember, you can control your breathing. Consciously, circle breathing is a much more efficient way to get oxygen into the bloodstream and to your muscles and brain with less energy expended.

Circle breathing gets its name from the circular pattern of breathing in through the nose and out through the mouth.

Picture your lungs as two balloons in your chest. The goal is to breathe slowly and evenly into the bottom of your lungs, and up to the top. When your lungs are filled, breathe out through your mouth slowly and evenly.

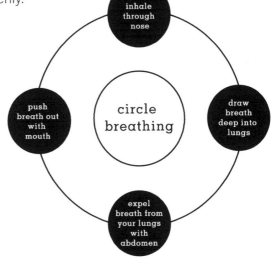

Focus Questions:

How can you use circle breathing to enhance your performance and how do you think it will give you an advantage over another player who doesn't practice it?

How can you use circle breathing when you're feeling overwhelmed emotionally?

104

Power Play Action Steps:

Describe how you feel mentally after five circle breaths...

Describe how you feel physically after five circle breaths...

Name a couple of situations in which using circle breathing could be beneficial to you...

The 4 R's: When to use Circle Breathing

Rhythm

When running long distances, such as cross country, or just training for your sport, use circle breathing to keep a rhythm. For instance, breathe in slowly, evenly and deeply for four steps, and then out slowly, evenly and deeply for four steps. The first few times you try this, it may seem impossible. But like anything else, with a little focus and effort, it will become second nature.

Recovery

While circle breathing will help you with your rhythm during long distances, shorter runs and quick sprints are not ideal to try to control your breathing during. Instead, after a few quick short bursts, your breathing will naturally be shallow and short, known as "catching your breath." Instead of several quick shallow breathes, use circle breathing to return your breathing rate to normal.

Relax

Remember how taking a circle breath in normal situations relax you just a little? In sports, emotions can run high and cause you to place your focus on things out of your control. A quick circle breath mentally and physically relaxes your mind and muscles.

Are you better at the technical skills of your sport when you are relaxed or tense?

Re–focus

In the Focus section, you came up with re–focusing cues. Circle breathing is a good "action" cue to remind yourself to re–focus your attention on the relevant cues. For instance, we know that focusing on the referee after a bad call is counter–productive to performance. However, during the heat of battle it's not easy to think logically about this. This is where circle breathing comes in handy. If you have practiced the skill and can recognize when you are upset or at a high level of anxiety, you can use circle breathing to relax, and make the best decision for the situation, returning your focus to relevant cues.

Long term Relaxation

You know how to circle breathe and know how to use it on the playing field. It is a great solution for a short term, quick relaxation. But what about a more sustained relaxation? Are you like a kid on Christmas Eve the night before a game: so excited for tomorrow's events that you have trouble sleeping? Or for an afternoon game you can't get your mind off of it all morning? Being able to relax is a necessary skill.

One of the best skills for this is Progressive Relaxation (PR). From a mind–body perspective, this is the best of both worlds.

Progressive relaxation is just like the name suggests, when done correctly it slowly and steadily relaxes your mind and body. You will progress through your body, relaxing one muscle group at a time. As we have established in previous lessons, circle breathing is a great skill to relax your body and mind, and you will use circle breathing as the basis of progressive relaxation techniques.

Progressive Relaxation exercise 1 (about 5 minutes)

Sit or lay down in a comfortable and quiet place. Close your eyes and take circle breaths. You will direct each in–breath to a body part.

Behind the eyes

Whole head like a balloon

Neck

Shoulders

Upper arms

Forearms

Hands

Chest

Torso

Hips

Thighs

Hamstrings

Calves

Ankles

Feet

Progressive Relaxation exercise 2 (about 10 minutes)

Follow the same steps as PR 1. This time however, tense each muscle group for 5 seconds on the in–breath, and completely let go and relax on the out breath.

Progressive Relaxation exercise 3 (about 12 minutes)

Follow the same steps as PR 2. This time, on each relax/out-breath, mentally say "As my muscles relax, my mind relaxes."

Using PR techniques, your mind and body will start to

"remember" the difference between tense and relaxed. As you

fully tense your muscles in PR 2, and move to letting go of that

tension, you will feel distinct sensations.

What sensations did you feel?

In PR 3, you start to mentally associate that tense –> relax sensation with the words and the breath. The short term goal is that you relax your mind and body the night before or day during competition. Another added benefit is that it will make circle breathing more effective over the long run.

Energizing

You can breathe and use relaxation techniques if anxiety gets too high. But what about it it's too low? From time to time, players need to get motivated and pumped up to perform. Here are a few techniques you can use to increase your energy when it's lower than optimal:

Positive Imagery – What pumps you up? A favorite player? Winning a trophy? See the next chapter for more in–depth information on positive imagery.

Past Peak Performance – In the Positive Mindset section, you recalled your Past Peak Performance. Remember how just going over that situation in your mind's eye made you feel? Use this to increase your energy if it becomes too low.

Positive Declaration – Remember that positive thoughts and words lead to positive actions! In the Positive Mindset level, you came up with a Positive Declaration, a statement that you know logically to be true. Use it for inspiration.

Positive Body Language – Remember that repeated positive actions lead to positive behavior. Stand tall to pump yourself up!

Goal-setting – Stay focused on the controllables; the factors that lead to success are what goal setting is all about. Think about your daily goals and just focus your attention and energy on accomplishing them. When you do, your motivation, confidence, and energy will increase, and move on to bigger things.

Multimedia – Listen to your favorite band or watch a highlight video before competition to get the juices flowing.

Finding and keeping your optimal emotional level

Emotional levels and anxiety are bound to fluctuate during training and competition. This is not a negative or positive thing alone, but can become either based on the athlete's mindset. Athletes who know how to control their emotions and use them to improve their performance give themselves the best chance to succeed.

As with anything, the first step to being able to control your emotions is to become aware of what affects them. Once you know that, you can decide what solutions you need to use to exert that control. The skills of circle breathing, progressive relaxation, and energizing can help in this area.

Antonio – Select soccer player

Antonio is a high–level defender, playing on the best team in the region, as well as the state team. He came to work with a sport psychology consultant to address a problem he was having that was getting worse over time: he would throw up before big games. The bigger the game, the more he would puke.

It started to work its way down to not wanting to eat before games. That became a problem for afternoon and early evening games. A whole day would pass with no nutrition, which, for obvious reasons would affect his performance. He had lost his starting spot and was in danger of being dropped from the team.

I knew that we needed to take a two-pronged approach: 1) Teach Antonio some relaxation techniques so that he could begin to have some control over his body, and 2) Determine what was making him so nervous in the first place.

The very first thing we did was to "re–learn" anxiety. I let Antonio know that anxiety is a good thing, and that we just needed him to harness it as positive energy. He liked this way of thinking and took to it right away. Next, I taught him circle breathing to learn to start to relax. We did Progressive Relaxation techniques 1, 2, and 3 for several weeks straight. That, in addition to positive focus and imagery, helped him a great deal. This helped him to be able to relax when the tension started to come on.

What made him so nervous was the fear of making a mistake that could cost his team the game. Not only that but he had a "yeller" for a coach, which only served to intensify his nerves. To address this, I had Antonio re-frame all of his negative thoughts (the things he did not want to have happen in the game) into positive thoughts (what he needed to do to be successful). This changed perception entering the game, coupled with breathing and relaxation techniques, allowed him to control his emotions, and enter matches with confidence.

During our time together, Antonio was cut from the team, and accepted a spot on the "B" team. I was very impressed with the attitude in which he accepted this demotion. His stated goal was to earn his way back on to the top team, which he did within three months. His ability to control his emotions was a big contributor to his achieving his goal.

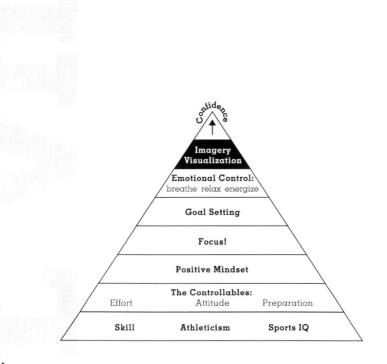

Confidence

Imagery Visualization

Emotional Control: breathe relax energize

Goal Setting

Focus!

Positive Mindset

The Controllables:
Effort   Attitude   Preparation

Skill   Athleticism   Sports IQ

Level VII – Visualization and Imagery

We are getting closer to the top of the pyramid. Visualization and imagery are the last steps to solidify in order to raise confidence to the highest possible level. In the Positive Mindset section, we said that athletes are, by nature, optimists. They see the success and have confidence that things will work out for the best. This includes how they envision the future.

Welcome back to the NCAA championship game. It's been a battle of the two best teams in the land today, and it all comes down to this: 5 seconds left, and Kentucky is down by 2 points to UCLA. The Wildcats set to inbound. The pass is made (5, 4...), return pass (3...), the shooter pump fakes and the defender goes flying (2…), shooter dribbles once to the left, sets his feet (1…), and let's fly with a 28 footer (*buzzer!*), and IT'S GOOOOODDD! Kentucky wins by one and is the national champion!

If you grew up in Kentucky, this was probably you at age 8, dreaming of leading your team to the crown. Little did you know back then, this was your first stab at visualization.

Many of us growing up daydreamed about hitting the winning shot or scoring the winning touchdown. Visualization is basically a controlled daydream. While visualization contains the word visual right in it, and makes you think of "seeing yourself" doing something, it is more than that. Visualization involves all the senses: sight, hearing, touch, taste, and smell.

Just as the young kid from Kentucky, many athletes continue this throughout their careers, and to great effect. As you will see in the next section, visualization is much more than just daydreaming: it's a way to build technical skills, engrain automatic responses to common situations in your sport, and to adjust your mindset. As this section progresses, you will learn how and why visualization works, how to conduct a successful visualization session, and some insights on imagery – which is using visual images to help you perform at a high level.

Why Visualization? Does it really work?

Have you ever had a nightmare? What happens to you physically when you have a bad dream? Sweating, screaming, sudden jolt to being awake, increased heart rate, and shallow rapid breathing can happen. Why? Because a monster was really chasing you? No! Your body doesn't know the difference between something really happening and your brain telling you something is happening. That mind–body connection is really strong. Imagine using that power for good – for your performance in sports.

There have been many studies over the years confirming the effectiveness of visualization on performance. In one study by a professor at the University of Chicago, basketball players were split into three groups:

Group 1 – Practiced shooting free throws an hour each day

Group 2 – Visualized themselves shooting free throws for an hour each day

Group 3 – Did not practice or visualize shooting free throws

The results?

Group 1 improved by 24%, Group 2 improved by 23%, and Group 3 did not improve at all. While visualization is no substitute for actual practice, it's pretty close! I wonder how a 4th group would have done visualizing for 30 minutes and shooting for 30 minutes…

Another similar study of golfers showed similar results. A group of college golfers was divided into three groups to develop their putting.

Group 1 – Just practiced putting

Group 2 – Just practiced visualizing putting: seeing and hearing the ball enter the hole

Group 3 – Practiced visualizing putting and seeing the ball track towards the hole only to have it veer away from the hole at the last second.

At the end of the study the golfers were tested on their putting an showed the following changes:

Group 1 – Improved 11%

Group 2 – Improved 30%

Group 3 – Declined 21%

Did you notice the difference in the two studies? The golf study introduced visualizing failure, which had devastating results to the athletes who did it. Not only does visualizing success help, but visualizing failure hurts performance. As a high level athlete, you have control of your thoughts (positive), your focus (controllables), your breathing (slow and even), and also your visualization (successful). But how do you do that?

How to Visualize 1: The four types of Visualization

"Muscle Memory"

When visualizing about your sport, your brain sends signals to your muscles similar to they way they do during the actual sport itself. So visualization helps your muscles "remember" how to move correctly.

From the base of the pyramid, what are the skills and techniques you need to work on?

118

Visualizing yourself doing these skills can help improve them tremendously.

"Automatic Response"

Practicing visualization can help you "see things before they happen," and develop an automatic response to situations that may arise in your sport. In sports, there is no time to think about what to do, you must trust your instincts, and that your body knows what to do. Practicing visualization of situations

that are likely to happen in your sport help to hone
your instincts.

For instance, if a basketball player has visualized not jumping
on an opponent's fake shot, when that situation occurs in the
game, he will have a better chance of not taking the fake.

Name a situation that arises in your sport frequently:

What is the best way to react to that situation?

"Mental Set"

Practicing visualization before competition can help you get in
the right frame of mind, whether you need to relax or energize.
Practice visualizing, with an emphasis on feeling confident
during competition.

*From the Emotional Control section, what is your Optimal Energy
level?*

Visualize yourself performing at that level. Using the Past Peak
Performance from Level 2 is a perfect way to start. So is using

the example of hitting the game winning shot at the beginning of this level.

"Recovery from Injury"

Injured athletes have some unique challenges. Using visualization when you can't physically perform is a great way to stay engaged and sharp. Leading up to the 1980 Summer Olympics, a heptathlete named Marilyn King injured her back in an accident. From her hospital bed, she visualized herself successfully performing her events for 6 months. In the trials, she was able to finish 2nd and qualify for the Olympics, having not physically trained for 6 months!

Visualizing your muscles, joints, and bones healing and back at full strength can be extremely helpful too.

When was the last time you were injured?

How could you have used visualization during that time?

How to Visualize 2: Best practices

Now you know how it works and why it's important, but how do you actually do it? Follow these steps:

Get in a comfortable place with no distractions (sitting or lying down are the best)

Breathe and relax (use circle breathing and possibly PR to relax the mind and body)

Control conditions: start by imagining the location and weather in full detail

Set the scene: specific event, opponents, teammates, coaches, fans, etc.

Include all the senses (sights, sounds, smells, tastes, touch)

Maximize vividness (it should look and feel as real as possible)

Be successful! (all visualization should be positive and successfully completed)

How to Visualize 3: The Specifics

Here are some other things to consider, to make visualization as effective as possible for you.

Viewpoint: Should I see myself from the stands, or visualize from my own eyes? Both can be effective, but for the most part, the internal view better engrains the feeling of the skill or situation.

Modeling: watch how your favorite player does a skill. Watch it closely then visualize yourself doing the skill.

Home movies: With visualization, you have control. You can slow down, pause, rewind, whatever you want to do to engrain the movement or attitude in your mindset.

Turn a negative into a positive: Have you ever made a mistake in a game and then gone over that situation a thousand times in your mind? What a way to take a mistake and code it into your central nervous system! Instead of reviewing the mistake, go over that same situation, but instead of the mistake, visualize how you could have been successful with it!

How often should I practice? This depends on the individual, but as with any other type of training, the key is to be consistent. Start with 5 minutes a day before practice, or before bed.

When should I practice? The best answer is before going to sleep at night – you are already lying down and comfortable. Plus it's a relaxing skill that can help you get rest. Not only that, but the last thing on your mind before sleeping is a positive thought of success. You can also visualize briefly before training, on the way to a game, or directly after competition.

Imagery

Imagery is often used interchangeably with visualization, but we will make a slight distinction between the two. Whereas visualization is putting yourself in a specific situation or practicing a certain skill, imagery is more about using images to harness the full power of your mentality. They say a picture is worth a thousand words. If that's true, then using a positive image is worth a thousand positive declarations. Use an image, a picture or video, that means specific things to you.

"She's quick as a cat!" "He can really jump out of the gym!" "When he gets going, he's like a runaway freight train." These are phrases we hear that relate an action to an image. The image we see makes us feel a certain way.

What's your favorite sport skill image?

Here are some examples I've seen some athletes use:

Lightning strike – A football player I worked with used the image of a lightning strike to accelerate to the ball in short bursts.

Stick of dynamite – In a dribbling drill, a soccer coach wanted his players to go from short winding dribbles through cones (slow pace) to a full sprint with the ball through the flags at the end. After telling his young players how to do this several times, he finally used the image of a stick of dynamite: "Dribble through the cones slowly like you've just lit a stick of dynamite. As you dribble through, the wick is burning down, and when you get to the last cone, 'explode' with speed through the flags, as the dynamite 'explodes.'" This image not only made the drill more fun for his kids, but it helped them achieve the level of intensity that the coach was looking for.

Tiger – A mixed martial arts fighter I worked with was a great grappler, but needed to work on getting her opponents to the ground so that she could utilize her skills. To get her to stop thinking so much and just use her instincts, I asked the athlete to come up with an image that embodied the actions she needed to take. For her, it was a tiger striking its prey. She enjoyed using this imagery to attack her opponents.

What are some images that remind you of skills in your sport?

What is a part of your game where you can use imagery to help enhance a skill?

Visualization and Imagery and the top of the Pyramid

The mind–body connection is so real, and the mind is so powerful, it would be a shame not to use it to your full potential for sport performance. Of course, you know that because you have not only bought this book, but you've made it this far! Using positive images can help your body remember. They can help your instincts improve to be sharp and ready. By thinking before the game, they can help you not have to think during the game.

Visualization Case Study
Adrianne – high school and select soccer player
Adrianne began working with a sport psychology consultant because she was returning to soccer after more than a year hiatus. During that time, she had dealt with injury and depression, but was worked her way through both and was ready to get back on the field to the game she loved.
She was a good technical player but her coach wanted her to be more physical, get into tackles more. We

started at the base of the pyramid – was she proficient in the skill? Did she know how to make tackles? She reported that she did, but was more scared about being injured again. She said she was usually not asked to be a tackler, so she didn't have much practice or experience, and if she did it wrong she may get hurt again.

To help her "remember" how to tackle, I lead her through some visualization exercises on getting into tackles. We set the scene, and had her "practice" slide tackles and hard challenges mentally. After one visualization session, she felt like she "knew how to do it." At our next session she was pleased to announce that she had made several tackles in practice and was looking forward to making a few in her upcoming tournament. Talk about going into competition with some confidence!

Confidence

Imagery
Visualization

Emotional Control:
breathe relax energize

Goal Setting

Focus!

Positive Mindset

The Controllables:

| Effort | Attitude | Preparation |

| Skill | Athleticism | Sports IQ |

Level VIII – Confidence

We have reached the top of the pyramid: Confidence. While the best of the best almost always have a natural confidence that never seems to leave them, the rest of us need to work at it. Like most things in life, a little maintenance goes a long way. To be confident, make habits out of those things that keep you confident.

Confidence is a belief in your abilities. Confidence is knowing what you have control over and directing your focus there. Confidence is being an optimist and thinking positive thoughts, saying positive things, and having positive habits. Confidence is having SMART goals and keeping up with them. Confidence is using anxiety and your emotions as energy. Confidence is visualizing success.

In short, confidence is a state of mind: a mindset. Performance can be based on your mindset as much as it can hinge on your physical state. As human beings, our mind state can change daily based on an infinite number of factors. Athletes who work on their Sports Mindset as much as they train physically find it easier to stay confident, no matter what factors may arise. Elite athletes know how to make the most out of their physical abilities by fully utilizing the sports mindset and playing with confidence. But just like the physical skills that can rust over time without proper training, the sports mindset takes consistent attention as well. To keep physically strong, you work out a couple times a week. To keep physically fit, you run or swim. To keep mentally strong and fit, work at it. Use this workbook to keep on top of it.

> **Always have goals!**
>
> **Focus on what you can control!**
>
> **Think, communicate, and act positively!**
>
> **Make sure your Angel is louder than your devil!**
>
> **Visualize success!**

Power Play Action Steps:

In the Introduction, you rated yourself on each skill in the SMP. Now that you've completed the workbook – answered all of the Focus Questions, completed the exercises, learned the skills, and taken the Power Play Action Steps – it's time to reflect. Take a moment to rate your strength for each level (1 being very weak and 10 being strong).

Now refer back to page 11 and compare.

Focus Questions:

Are there any areas in which your mental game are stronger now?

How did you improve in each area?

132

Are there any areas that your mental game still needs work?

What is the game plan to keep the strong areas strong and to improve the weaker areas?

Playing with confidence is no accident. And it's not something to hope comes to you in the big moments. Just like the physical skills in your sport, confidence and the mental game improve and grow when you dedicate yourself to them. Now you have the tools, so make the Sports Mindset part of your everyday game plan.

About the Author

Brian Baxter, MA is a sport psychology consultant, soccer coach and all–around sports enthusiast living in Portland, OR. As the Director of Sport Psychology Institute Northwest, Brian is dedicated to helping athletes reach their peak performance and confidence on a more consistent basis. He works with athletes of all sports and skill levels regularly, and presents workshops to teams, coaches, parents and organizations.

If you're not meeting with Brian in a sport psychology setting, you will most likely find him with his wife Debbie, and sons Hawk and Zavier on a soccer field, in the outdoors or cheering with the Timber's Army at Jeld–Wen Field.

About Sport Psychology Institute Northwest (SPINw)

For a decade, we have successfully worked with athletes, parents, and coaches to provide solutions to questions like: Do you want to take control of your confidence, learn how to focus, and develop a consistent performance? Are you in a slump, or want to prevent a long slump? Do you get too nervous before games, or lose yourself in the emotional storms of your mind? Our team of consultants are accomplished competitive athletes with specialized sport psychology training, committed to passing on their experience to you through one–on–one coaching, group and team seminars, and online education.

For more information, please visit our website – www.spinw.com

Find us on Facebook –

http://www.facebook.com/SportPsychologyInstituteNW

Follow our Twitter feed – @SPINw

Made in the USA
San Bernardino, CA
07 March 2014